I WANT TO PRAY BUT...

Published by
Messenger Publications,
37, Lower Leeson Street,
Dublin 2.

With ecclesiastical permission,
Dublin 1978.

ISBN 1 872245 32 3
3-1-93
2-5-95

I Want to Pray but...

JOHN HYDE, S.J.

MESSENGER PUBLICATIONS

LORD, TEACH US TO PRAY

We ask you, God of grace and eternal life, to make us share in the prayer of Jesus. He is the great worshipper of God in spirit and in truth, he is the mediator through whom alone our prayer can reach to the throne of grace. We wish to pray in him, united with his prayer. May he teach us to pray. May he teach us to pray as he himself prayed, to pray at all times and not to give up, to pray perseveringly, confidently, humbly, with true love of our neighbour without which no prayer is pleasing to you. May he teach us to pray for what he prayed: that your name may be hallowed, your will be done, your Kingdom come among us; for only if we first pray in that way, praising and thanking you, will you also hear us when we pray for ourselves, our earthly well-being and our earthly cares . . . .

Karl Rahner, S.J.

COULD YOU HELP ME PLEASE?

There is someone already helping you to pray. The Holy Spirit is in your heart. Your Father who is in heaven sent him. And your Brother sent him. He knows what is suitable for you to say. In summary, he gets you to pray: 'Father'.

By the Holy Spirit you have faith, so that you can say 'Yes' to what Christ taught us. By the Holy Spirit you have hope, relying on God. By the Holy Spirit you have charity, so that you value God above all, and you love his whole family for love of him.

In the Gospel the disciples asked our Lord to teach them to pray. His answer was the 'Our Father'. They then had the 'Our Father' as an outline, filled in with our Lord's own example. You inherit that. From our Lord you know who your Father is, and what he is like, and how greatly he loves you. From our Lord you know that you will be listened to.

Your mother taught you to pray. Behind your mother was your holy Mother, the Church, Christ's Church, directed by the Holy Spirit. The Church is always teaching you about Christ, and about his

Father and your Father. Through the Mass and the Sacraments, the Church is always getting you to pray. Christ's command is being carried out: 'Teach all nations'.

You cannot be helped to pray unless you pray; no more than you can be helped to walk unless you walk. Perseverance is needed, too; keep at it. All worthwhile things are acquired slowly. One's education takes years; so does prayer.

I am not helping you directly, but only pointing out helps which are already there, as a bus-guide does. A more personal guide is useful, to whom you could tell (as you go on) what you did and failed to do about your prayer. If you seek such a guide, the Lord will provide one for you.

And so you pray

O my God, you are very good to me. You made me for your company. You provided all that is needed, with help and encouragement. Give me, also, now the good will not to be making difficulties about talking to you, but to plunge into it.

PRAYER MEANS NOTHING TO ME NOW

What others say influences you more than you like to admit. Their value-judgment saying: 'Such a thing is no good', makes an impact, especially if it rushes at you with the force and weight of television; it dents the natural curve of your bonnet. Of course, it is good and necessary that we be influenced by others. But there is good influence and bad influence.

Suppose you left long ago the place where you were born, you might say, 'That place means nothing to me now'. You mean: 'I do not wish to go back there; I do not look for news from there, no emotion or interest is aroused in me by the sight or mention of it'. Well, one can live satisfactorily after being transplanted. It would not be the same if you said; 'My father and mother mean nothing to me now'. The connection there is lasting. If you said; 'God means nothing to me now', it would show a defect in you greater than forgetting your father and mother, because the connection is more lasting and far deeper. Away from God, you cannot live satisfactorily at all; though you may think you can.

God made you for God. Other things, your native place, your father and mother, husband or wife, may be taken from you, and you can still get on. But without God it is no life. This is true even when you think it is not. To wake up and see that you had chosen to throw away God for evermore would be hell.

You can change your mind now about your father and mother. Under the influence of a friend or relative you can come back to them in your heart. Such influence would be good. The value-judgment behind it is true. The bend it makes in you restores the suitable curve. It is a healthy influence; open yourself to it.

Prayer is your dealing with God, like writing to your father and mother. If it means nothing to you, why? Think again.

And so you pray

Lord, that I may see. I let myself be blinded about you. I am sorry. I beg pardon for making so little of you and your goodness. Open my eyes to what is truly good. Open my heart to you.

COULD YOU HELP ME TO PRAY BETTER?

It is better to pray better. The young person who has little time for father and mother is not good. God's children are meant for the happy company of our Father who is in heaven and ought to be always in touch with him. 'One ought to pray always and never stop'.

You pray better if the defects in your prayer are lessened. When someone is speaking to you whom you greatly respect and love, you take care of little courtesies, position of your body, attention, according to the situation. In prayer you are answering God, for God is trying to speak to you all the time; so it is for you to take care of courtesy.

Distractions which you cannot help are a defect you have to put up with. Courtesy demands that you come back to God promptly when you catch yourself wandering away, and that you sincerely beg pardon for any wandering which was your fault. A focus for attention can help — a picture, a word or phrase, a symbol.

When you really want something, you allow no

distractions. This is obvious when you are praying for a dear one who is dying. What do you want in prayer? do you want it only mildly, caring little whether you get it or not? The principal thing that is to be got by prayer is God; how much do you want God? See if the defect in your prayer is here.

A tape reciting a prayer to another tape is obviously not prayer. To pray, you need to be in it, personally, as well as you can. God has to be in it too. It is a defect in prayer to be all taken up with yourself and your side of the conversation.

There are things which you learn to do by doing them once or a few times. Other things need long practice. Prayer needs all your life. Watch for the defects and lessen them. Keep improving, even when you seem to be getting worse. It is worth it.

And so you pray

Lord, make me genuine. I beg your pardon for being half-hearted with you. You are patient with me, where another would turn away from me in disgust. My heart is in your hand; make me whole-hearted.

NOTHING HAPPENS WHEN I PRAY

You mean that nothing happens from God's side. In prayer we labour, and we rely on God to do what is beyond our power to do. What God does then is what is in question here.

God is invisible. If then, because you do not see him, you say he is not there, your judgment is mistaken. He is like a kind benefactor who takes care that you do not see him. But with God, in the nature of things, you have ways of knowing that he is there and who he is; so you can correct your judgment. You know that in prayer you are not talking to nobody.

God's action is somewhat invisible too. What happens to you is from the hand of God, though you can mistakenly judge that it is not. Of the changes God makes in you by his smiling favour, some cannot be noticed by you; some can be noticed, but can be put down by you to other causes. Much of this you can find out by reasoning and Faith; not till the Last Day will you know all he did. The kind benefactor left enough traces of himself to woo your love.

Your mistaken judgments, in so far as they are innocent, will be got over one way or another by his wooing. In so far as they are your choosing — none so blind as they who will not see — they cannot be got over unless you choose to reverse your choice. That means setting yourself to learn, re-considering.

You have to develop an eye for certain things or you do not see them. In ordinary life everyone knows that. If I see no significance in a certain chain of events, that might be because I did not develop the eye. The eye for seeing what happens when you pray is given by God. But it needs developing.

God said: 'Ask and you shall receive'. That is enough for me. If I do not see anything coming, I know all the same that something is coming. If what I see coming seems to be the wrong thing, I know who it is I am dealing with, and I trust him. Even if I never see till the Last Day, I am satisfied to wait, since it is he for whom I wait.

And so you pray

Lord, give me the grace to plod on, even in gloom. I beg your pardon for mis-judging you. I ought to know that you are good. Help me to trust you all the way.

8

ISN'T IT BETTER TO WORK FOR OTHERS THAN TO PRAY?

A person is helped when he is made better by what is done for him. He is hungry; you feed him, and so make him better. Let that stand also for the many other things you might do for others to help them.

A man is right when he is turned to God. Let him be well fed and not turned to God and he is not right. Hungry and turned to God he is right in the main thing.

Normally, you begin feeding him, if you can, and then come to the 'turning to God'. He more easily turns to God when he is fed. You are ready and eager to say more about this point, so I leave it to you.

Yet it happens not uncommonly that the hungry man turns to God on account of his hunger and the well-fed man turns away from God on account of being well fed. (Remember that we are talking also about other things you might do to help, feeding the hungry being only one instance.) Indeed, the cry of distress is a rather typical prayer in the Bible; typical too is. 'He sent the rich empty away', as the *Magnificat* says.

Only God can turn a man to God. You can help from the outside, putting reasons or considerations, blowing away prejudice, arranging some circumstances; and you hope that God will do the rest. God arranged for you to share in his work in the world in that way. He arranged that you share by prayer also, 'Give us this day . . .'. The prayer asks God to do what we cannot do.

A man is turned to God when he is praying. A much more thorough turning is needed, no doubt, so he may keep on praying. He benefits by your praying, because there is some sharing among God's children. So maybe you might re-consider the purpose and scope of your work for others.

And so you pray

Father in heaven, give us our daily bread. Give me also the grace to put first things first, and not to put baker's bread before the Bread that you give for the life of the world. You are what we need most of all.

I NEVER FEEL GOD IS NEAR WHEN I TRY TO PRAY

If you persevere in praying, something happens. It may not be what you expected. Yet it is more valuable than what you expected.

It is wonderful to feel that God is near. It can do you much good, helping your courage, and convincing you that there are better things than what the eye sees.

Yet God has to take that feeling away from you. If you thought that prayer was first of all for your satisfaction, you would be mistaken. God made you such that one day you could be really satisfied with what is really satisfying. But to think that God is there just for your satisfaction, and not rather that you are there for God, would be a mistake; it is not so. Mistake would spoil the satisfaction. Deep friendship cannot be built on error. So God has to disillusion you; he has to set you right.

When you do not feel that God is near, he is near all the same. And you know that he is near, not by feeling but by Faith. In prayer, it is enough that God is near and that you know.

The feeling that God is near is not reliable. God is still near when the feeling is gone. When you feel that he is not near but far, he is still near. He has to teach you that it is not by feeling that you know him.

Even if you never feel that God is near when you try to pray, you can still pray, And your prayer can be what it ought to be. By it you can honour God, and that is what we are for. By it God can change you, removing the illusion and the crookedness that spoils you, turning you towards your true love.

And so you pray

Lord, turn me to you. I want to turn to you now in prayer. But I am turned in on myself partly—maybe mostly—and that is not right. Lord, my true love, give me to see clearly that I am not the centre of all.

MY WORDS TO HEAVEN GO, MY THOUGHTS REMAIN BELOW

It is fitting that your thoughts be often on your family. Even when you pray, and your words are addressed to God, your strong interest in your family will keep your thoughts, much of the time, on your family. The same holds for whatever your interest is, lasting or passing.

Yet for the good of your family your thoughts need to go to God too. You might call a doctor for one of your family, or you might want them to meet this person or that for their good; much more do you need to go to God about them. Need, according as you realize it, drives you. Then later you come to see that God is more than even your family. This change in you can be slow.

You can be dealing with customers in a shop all day for the sake of your family, to support them. Your work can demand your whole thought, so that during work you cannot think of your family. But your 'heart' is with your family, meaning your will, the intention that keeps you working. In prayer your thoughts are below in spite of you, it can still be that

13

your 'heart' is in Heaven with your words, if it is really for God that you are praying.

What is keeping you praying? Thought about God is important, assimilating what you know about God by Faith. Without it you are not well nourished, and prayer will be weak. But a stage can come when you know very well that God is there and that He is the best, and that is why you are praying, yet think of Him you cannot (almost). Your mind may then wander below most of the time in spite of you, but an important part of you is above, the more important for this purpose, and your prayer is good.

And so you pray

Lord, I have to go now to my work. I consecrate my work to you. You are the main reason for it. Give me the grace to do nothing in it that would come between me and you. And give me an undivided heart so that I may work really for you.

WHAT WILL BE WILL BE

That was a Spanish song. What it says is true. But what you are reading into is not true. It does not follow that to ask God for anything is silly.

You read into the song here a statement that God is like a great machine with big wheels turning inexorably, crushing . . . . What will be will be. Stop. Your statement is false. God is not like that. God is wise. God is good. God made you free. Now, control your imagination with good sense and Faith.

If you drive a car through a busy street in a certain drunken condition, harm will be done. In the lawcourt afterwards you may plead: 'what will be will be', to escape free. The court will tell you that harm would not have been done IF you had not chosen to drive in that condition. What will be will be, IF . . . . And what will not be will not be, IF . . . .

What happens in this world happens in God's plan. God's plan includes your foolish decision or wise decision and all the other causes and circumstances. Your prayer is included.

My planning could not include so much. Your

15

petition would take my by surprise, so that I would have to refuse you or adjust my plan or admit that I could not manage. God is not small like I am. God's plan covers all, all, including your prayer.

It is not pointless to have you asking. God could not make a world where our daily bread would not come from God — through the sweat of our brow, no doubt. Children ask, and then in time they grow up and ask no longer; children who could do for themselves would be no children. But creatures do not grow up to do without God.

Home is beautiful and happy. It is a picture of Heaven with our eldest brother in the centre. He says to our Father: 'All I have is from you'. This does not spoil the happiness but rather perfects it. And it will be, IF we say: 'Give us this day our daily bread'.

And so you pray

O my God, help me not to be fooled or even delayed by clever reasonings but to love what is truly good, so that I may do each time what you desire for me, and so come home in the end.

I HAVE GIVEN UP BUT I WANT TO PRAY

God is drawing you back. The negative going away is our doing; the positive coming back is our doing but mostly God's doing. God turns you to God. Many fathers and mothers are crying at the present time, longing for their children to come back; God is like them, only that God has more ways of working.

Through Mass and the Sacraments you keep contact with God and God with you. Refuse to travel that road and contact is difficult.

Mass and the Sacraments are a school of prayer. By doing what is involved in them, you are practising prayer and learning prayer. We are slow learners. In the matter of prayer we are never finished school.

Prayer frees you and opens you to God, so that when God speaks, you can hear, when God draws, you can be drawn. After prayer is given up, it is hard for God to get in a word.

That you are in want means that you are being drawn. When you find that you are being drawn, you can say: 'No' or you can say: 'Yes'. The son far away can burn the letter from home. At this moment you can say 'Yes' to God.

That you ask what you ought to do means that you are saying: 'Yes'. Some of those who heard St Peter's first sermon asked the same question. You could then draw back, refusing to do what you were told, counting the price too big to pay for the pearl. Or you could let yourself be drawn on, admitting that the pearl is priceless, counting no price too much.

What ought you do? Pray. You can, because you are being drawn. Go over the lessons you learnt. 'Our Father who art in Heaven'; 'O God, be merciful to me a sinner'; 'Holy Mary, pray for us sinners'. Keep at it.

And so you pray

O my Saviour, carry back the lost sheep on your shoulders. Yes, I want to let you carry me. I want to get home, to you and our Father who is in heaven.

MY PRAYER SEEMS UESLESS –
I AM NO BETTER THAN I EVER WAS

In a difficult climb there can be times when to hold your own and not slip back is progress. If you were not praying, you could be slipping back. Prayer is keeping you steady, poised for a new effort.

Progress is not always easy to judge. As you move on, you see faults to which you were blind before. You see more dirt in a dim and dirty room as the light increases. What seemed nothing before, now is seen to be very bad. For such reasons you could judge that you got worse whereas you got better.

We want and we do not want the same thing. You want to be cured of a certain ailment, and for years you refuse to use the cure prescribed for you, though you are most willing to use other cures. You may be acting that way now about your spiritual health. A needless occasion of sin not avoided could be holding you back. You could develop convenient blindness to that in time.

It is always a case of wanting and not wanting God. Of course, you want God, but you want something else too, and often enough you cannot have both.

Where it is a choice of two people whom you think of marrying, each being wonderfully good, you know that you have to make up your mind. Here the something else is very good, made by God; but God is altogether better, and you cannot do without him; and, as it is now, you cannot have both; so make up your mind.

The practical conclusion from what you said is not: 'Give up praying', but: 'Give up measuring your progress by unsuitable standards, and examine your sincerity, and go on praying'.

And so you pray

O my God, give me the grace to care about you more, so that nothing then can compete with you for my heart. Time spent with you is well spent anyhow. For you are the best.

I FEEL A HYPOCRITE WHEN I PRAY

The hypocrites condemned in the Gospel were wrong because their main purpose was to be seen by men, not to be seen by God. Men see what shows outside, God sees the heart. Since the real purpose of prayer is to come to God, talking to God and listening to him in your heart; and prayer which neglects that is no good. This is not seen by men, but only by God who sees in secret into your heart. The outer gesture and attitude of prayer, which men see, could be there without the inner thing, and then, if that is your choice, you are a hypocrite.

It is often better to close the door and be seen by no one when you pray, because your tendency to show off gets no play then. Sometimes it is better to pray in sight of others, as you do at Mass, or as contemplatives in a monastery do in a guarded way. Let your light shine before men, so far as it may help them and not hinder you in glorifying our Father who is in Heaven. But also, when you pray, close the door.

At Mass or wherever else you are seen by others,

you may attend to what you are doing. As it is not good then to be admiring or criticising your neighbour's hat, so it is not good to be concerned more than you need with what others see or think. What you are doing is about God and for God. In so far as you can, attend to God.

For various reasons you may not succeed always in attending to God. Distraction can come and take away your attention in spite of you. In that case, you give to God all you can at the time, namely that outer attention which is still in your power and which neighbours also can see. Your heart is still right in purpose. It is for that reason that you give God the time and make your hands and your lips praise him. If then the inner attention is missing and you cannot help it, that is not hypocrisy, no matter what you feel.

And so you pray

O God, you see the heart. You see in my heart too much hypocrisy. But I am at this prayer for you rather than for men. At least, I want it to be so. And I beg of you a clean heart, intent on you above all.

HOW CAN PRAYER END VIOLENCE

I do not know. I cannot tell you all God's ways. When you pray, you meet someone who is above you. It is not that you know nothing about him; he made known to you what you need to know for the present. You know that he is there, and that he made all, that he knows all, that he directs and governs all, and that he is good. But you do not know everything about him; far from it. On the last day at the Judgment He will show us what he did. Until then, we know little.

So, respect and modesty are called for in prayer, indeed, deep reverence. What Job learnt has to be learnt by all of us. There is a sense in which you cannot question God. Refuse to be modest before God, and prayer becomes unreal. A critic or accuser of God cannot pray, no more than he can love. That is how to destroy any true love.

Suppose one of your family is doing something seriously wrong. Let us say it is unjust violence. He will not listen to you when you point out to him how wrong it is. Neither will he listen to friends. You turn to God.

What is God to do? I can think out what it is for a man to be free in his choices, and how he can be influenced, and even how God might influence him since God has control of all influences. But how in fact the man will respond to such and such an influence I do not know. And what God is to do is not for me to say. I pray. I beg. I appeal. I know that nothing is impossible with God.

You are right to turn to God. God is our Shepherd and we are sheep of his flock. The heart of a man is in the hand of God. 'Our Father, do not let us give in to temptation but deliver us from evil'.

And so you pray

O Saviour of mankind, that brother of mine who is on the downward slope, rescue him. You taught us to pray: bring about that we do not give in to temptation. I am saying that prayer for him now. In this matter all that I can do is to beg you to do what is needed. I adore and beg and leave all to you.

WHAT CHRIST OUR LORD SAID

ABOUT PRAYER

When you pray, go into your room and shut the door and pray to your Father who is in secret; and your Father who sees in secret will reward you. Mt. 6:6.

And in praying do not heap up empty phrases . . . for your Father knows what you need before you ask him. Mt. 6:7.

When you pray, say: Father, hallowed be thy name. Thy Kingdom come, thy will be done, on earth as it is in heaven. Give us each day our daily bread; and forgive us our sins, as we also have forgiven our debtors; and lead us not into temptation but deliver us from evil. Mt. 6:9-13; Lk 11:2-4.

And whenever you stand praying, forgive if you have anything against any one; so that your Father also, who is in heaven, may forgive you your trespasses. Mk. 11:25.

Do not be anxious, saying, 'What shall we eat?' or 'What shall we drink?' or 'What shall we wear?' . . . your heavenly Father knows that you need them all. Instead, seek his Kingdom and these things shall be yours as well. Mt. 6:31-32; Lk 12:31.

I tell you, have faith in God; whatever you ask in prayer, believe that you will receive it, and you will. Mk. 11:24; Mt. 17:20.

Not every one who says to me, 'Lord, Lord', shall enter the Kingdom of heaven, but he who does the will of my Father who is in heaven. Mt. 7:21; Lk. 6:46-49.

And I tell you, ask and it will be given you; seek and you will find; knock, and it shall be opened to you. Lk. 11:5-13.

I say to you, if two of you agree on earth about anything they ask, it will be done for them by my Father in heaven. For where two or three are gathered in my name, there am I in the midst of them. Mt. 18:19-20.

RECOMMENDED READING

NEW

J45   **Day by Day in Prayer - 1**
J46   **Day by Day in Prayer - 2**
by Canice Egan, S.J.

These little booklets are an attempt to express some age-old spiritual truths as a help to prayer. They are offered to members of prayer-groups and others who wish to spend some time each day in quiet prayer.

ALSO

J38   **Listening to Silence**
by Canice Egan, S.J.

A beautifully illustrated prayer booklet with colourful, contemplative photographs.